Managing the International Assignment Process

From Selection Through Repatriation

ROGER HEROD

GLOBAL HR MANAGEMENT SERIES

Expatriate Compensation
The Balance-Sheet Approach

Short-Term International Assignments
Implementing Effective Policies

Global Compensation and Benefits
Developing Policies for Local Nationals

Expatriate Compensation Strategies
Applying Alternative Approaches

International Assignment Programs
Tackling the Critical Issues

Benchmarking International Assignment Programs
Assessing Overall Effectiveness

Managing the International Assignment Process
From Selection Through Repatriation

About the Author

Roger Herod, SPHR, is a senior vice president of ORC, based in its Chicago office. He is responsible for ORC's worldwide expatriate consulting services and carries out a wide range of global projects for major multinational clients both in the United States and Europe.

Herod has held senior-level international human resources positions since 1974 and has worked extensively in the United States, Europe, Latin America and the Far East. He has worked for such leading companies as Procter & Gamble, General Foods, R.J. Reynolds and Campbell Soup, where he was vice president, human resources, for Campbell Soup's International Division.

Herod has served on the board of directors of SHRM's HR Certification Institute and has been extensively involved in developing the Global Professional in Human Resources Certification program. He speaks at a wide range of seminars and conferences and is the editor of the *International Human Resources Guide*. He also has had articles published in various journals, including *Benefits and Compensation International* and *Mobility*.

Herod is a graduate of Manchester University in the United Kingdom and is a Chartered Fellow of the United Kingdom Institute of Personnel Management and Development. He has lived and worked in the United Kingdom, Belgium and Switzerland, as well as the United States.

The Society for Human Resource Management (SHRM) is the world's largest professional association devoted to human resource management. Our mission is to serve the needs of HR professionals by providing the most current and comprehensive resources, and to advance the profession by promoting HR's essential, strategic role. Founded in 1948, SHRM represents members in over 140 countries, and has a network of more than 575 affiliated chapters in the United States, as well as offices in China and India. Visit SHRM at www.shrm.org.

Interior and Cover Design: Shirley E.M. Raybuck
Library of Congress Cataloging-in-Publication Data

Herod, Roger, 1944-
  Managing the international assignment process : from selection through repatriation / Roger Herod.
      p. cm. -- (Global HR management series)
    ISBN 978-1-58644-150-0
    1. International business enterprises--Personnel management. 2. Employment in foreign countries. I. Title.
    HF5549.5.E45H4697 2009
    658.3--dc22
                                                    2009008190
  10 9 8 7 6 5 4 3 2 1

Contents

About the Series

This is the seventh and final book in a series of publications that have been developed on different aspects of Global Human Resources Management. The first two books—*Expatriate Compensation* and *Short-Term International Assignments*—covered the most typical approaches used by companies to compensate employees transferred on international assignments ranging from three months to five years. The third—*Global Compensation and Benefits*—covered the issues involved in developing effective compensation and benefits policies for individuals employed in different countries on local terms and conditions. The fourth and fifth books—*Expatriate Compensation Strategies* and *International Assignment Programs*—dealt with the increasingly wide range of different approaches to international assignment policies and the critical issues faced by companies in managing their assignment programs. The sixth—*Benchmarking International Assignment Programs*—addressed the issues involved both in assessing the external competitiveness of assignment policies and obtaining feedback on the program's effectiveness through satisfaction surveys of assignees and managers. Throughout this book, reference is made to competitive data on the latest international assignment policies and practices among multinational companies from *ORC's 2008 Worldwide Policies and Practices Survey* in which 930 global multinationals participated.

Introduction

The success of any global mobility program depends on a series of complex and interlinked processes. These processes include not only developing an attractive compensation package, but also selecting a candidate with the appropriate technical and intercultural skills, providing comprehensive relocation and settling-in assistance to the assignee and family, dealing with the inevitable issues that arise during the assignment, and establishing an effective career management and repatriation (or next assignment) planning process. Although compensation is always important, family issues have proved for many years to be the most common reason for assignment failure. What may seem to be a very attractive career opportunity can turn into a nightmare if the spouse and children are unable to adapt to the assignment location.

Global mobility programs have become increasingly critical to the success or failure of many companies' global business development initiatives. This requires having the appropriate resources available to be able to deploy where needed. The first step in the process is to be able to identify candidates for international assignments with the necessary technical and cultural skills. However, experience shows that being able to provide both assignees and their families with the support services they need during the relocation process—on assignment and during repatriation—is at least as important.

The following comments from Jack Welch, the former CEO of GE, provide an interesting perspective on the importance of global mobility:

> *"The Jack Welch of the future cannot be like me. I spent my entire career in the U.S. The next head of General Electric will be somebody who spent time in Bombay, in Hong Kong, in Buenos Aires.*

We have to send our brightest and best overseas and make sure they have the training that will allow them to be the global leaders who will make GE flourish in the future."

Welch's comments illustrate the critical need for top management commitment and support in using international assignments to help develop global leaders. This effort requires ongoing top management involvement in deciding which employees are selected for assignments, monitoring their performance on assignment, and ensuring that their newly acquired international skills and talents are properly used upon repatriation. Without this level of top management support, employers can find themselves with frustrated and demoralized assignees that feel they are "out of sight, out of mind" while on assignment, and are left to their own devices to find their next job in the company, with the inevitable result that many leave the company within two-to-three years after repatriation.

Ultimately, the most powerful message a company can convey is to state publicly that employees will not be considered for top management positions unless they have had international assignment experience.

Global Mobility Strategy

International HR managers have a crucial role to play in establishing an effective global mobility strategy. This role involves considerably more than developing and administering assignment policies and programs. In order to gain acceptance as true business partners, HR managers need to meet with senior business managers that have responsibility for the company's international business operations on a regular basis in order to:

- Gain a thorough understanding of the company's global business needs.
- Assess where critical skills and talents will be needed globally.
- Identify potential resources within the organization.
- Help develop global mobility staffing plans and policies to meet business needs.
- Develop policies that enable the company to deploy resources globally in a cost-effective manner.

HR managers should challenge the temptation to fill every business need with an expensive expatriate relocation by proposing alternative and creative solutions. The issues involved in deploying talent on a global basis have become increasingly complex, so that "one-size-fits-all" assignment policies are rarely appropriate today within major multinationals. More and more companies are questioning why they have a large and costly inventory of long-term assignees who are not particularly high-potential and for whom it is difficult to find a suitable position upon repatriation. To meet the company's global business requirements, HR managers need to be able to design and manage a complex series of different policies and staffing strategies—commuter assignments, short-term assignments, developmental assignments, regional assignments, the more traditional two-to-five year assignments, localization, and other specialized types of policies where needed.

Key Processes

Selection

In an ideal world, companies have a pool of candidates ready, willing, and able to be considered for international assignments. The employer then chooses candidates who have the right technical and intercultural skills, as well as families who are excited about the prospect of spending the next three or four years in Guangzhou, China or Bangalore, India. Unfortunately, very few companies have such a talent pool. Despite all the evidence about the importance of selecting candidates with the right intercultural skills, most decisions regarding who to send on international assignments continue to be made by business managers on the basis of technical competence and job performance.

Selection	
What are the most important factors in selecting employees for international assignments?	
	% of companies
Technical skills or competencies	66%
Job Performance	25%
ORC 2008 Worldwide Policies and Practices Survey—930 participants Copyright © 2008, ORC Worldwide	

In general, companies seem reluctant to make judgments about the potential cultural adaptability of candidates for international assignments—especially their families—despite survey data showing that family issues and inability to adapt to the host location are the top reasons for assignment failure. The most likely explanation for this hesitation is that companies are generally concerned about turning a candidate down on what could be perceived as somewhat subjective and possibly unfair grounds; they may feel safer basing their selection decisions on more easily defended factors such as technical skills and job performance.

What can be done to take potential cultural adaptability factors into account? Providing candidates and their spouses/partners the opportunity to meet with a third-party consultant or psychologist who has extensive international experience can be very beneficial. In addition, employers should encourage candidates and their spouses/partners to take self-assessment tests to gain insight into their potential cultural adaptability, such as the Overseas Assignment Inventory, Culture Shock Inventory, or GlobeSmart Candidate Assessment Profile. This combination of counseling and tests will certainly raise awareness among candidates and their families of the challenges they will face. In some cases, this realization may cause candidates to turn down the assignment voluntarily, which is certainly preferable to the risk of costly assignment failure.

Career Planning—Pre-Assignment

All too often, HR managers find themselves confronted with urgent requests from line managers who are trying to resolve an immediate business need or crisis through an international assignment. They have already identified a potential candidate and have little interest in anything beyond getting the employee and family on a plane as quickly as possible. What can HR managers do to minimize the likelihood of these types of situations? Here are some useful strategies that various companies have implemented:

- Get proactively involved by holding quarterly meetings with the heads of major business areas to review not only potential business projects that might require international assignees, but also performance and repatriation plans for current assignees.
- Establish a policy requiring business managers who propose potential international assignments to submit a written business justification for top management approval that includes the scope and length of the proposed assignment, as well as a cost projection to justify the investment. This requirement ensures that each request is properly reviewed and approved in advance. Insisting on this level of scrutiny frequently

results in the need for assignments to be reconsidered or alternative candidates to be identified.

- Use an assignment initiation form that specifies the proposed length of the assignment, individual's job title, reporting structure, and repatriation plans. Employers may also specify a career mentor for the assignee, preferably a senior manager in the same business field.
- Incorporate specific career plans in the letter of assignment provided to the assignee, including assignment duration and plans for repatriation or localization if the assignee wishes to remain in the host country.
- Where possible, provide a repatriation letter to assignees, the host-country manager, and the manager to whom they will report upon return. This approach is ideal; however, rapidly changing business environments and needs make it very difficult for most companies to make this level of commitment on a regular basis.

Whatever the specific assignment planning and approval system used, experience shows that the more thought given to the need for the assignment and longer-term career plans for the assignee, the better the chance of a successful investment for both company and employee.

> "Most U.S. firms make global assignments primarily on the basis of the needs of a given position and their inability to fill it with a host-country employee. In the day-to-day reality of the decision-makers responsible for global assignments, succession planning and management development are often irrelevant."
> —(Globalizing People through International Assignments.)
> J. Stewart Black, Hal B. Gregersen, Mark E. Mendenhall, Linda K. Stroh

Relocation Support

Pre-Assignment Trip

Before candidates are expected to make a final decision about an assignment, over 80 percent of North American and European multinationals organize a pre-assignment visit to the host location for the potential assignee and spouse/partner, sometimes including any children as well. This critical step in the relocation process provides an opportunity to better understand the pros and cons of the location, meet future colleagues, and, if possible, spend time with other assignees and their families at the location working for the company. Employers usually allow five to seven days for the visit and reimburse all expenses.

If possible, it is highly advisable to use a knowledgeable relocation firm to arrange a briefing about the location and facilities for assignees and families. If children are going abroad, the firm would also arrange visits to schools.

As assignees often use the pre-assignment trip for house hunting to find a suitable rental property, HR needs to carefully manage this step and coordinate it with a relocation firm. Before any house hunting takes place, HR should establish clear guidelines as to the type of property and rental limit for which the company is willing to pay—and then communicate this information to the assignee and the relocation firm to avoid misunderstandings. Unfortunately, problems frequently occur when HR has not given clear instructions to relocation firms, who then show rental properties to assignees that are well in excess of the company's cost guidelines. Having to explain to a potential assignee and spouse/partner that the company is not willing to cover the costs of the "dream house" they have found is a very negative start to any assignment. (Housing is further discussed later in this book.)

Immigration and Work Permits
Before the assignee and family can relocate to the host country, there are some important legal issues that need to be addressed. Before arriving in the host country, both the assignee and family members must obtain residence visas, the costs of which are normally borne by the employer. In addition, the assignee needs a work permit for most countries. Depending on the particular country regulations, the processing time to obtain a work permit can range from one month to six months or more.

Delays in securing appropriate visas and work permits are frustrating for the company, as well as the assignee and family. However, attempts to circumvent the rules by pretending that the assignee is on a temporary business trip can be fraught with risk and may even jeopardize the company's business status in the host country. Information sharing between government departments (e.g., immigration, tax services) and between governments themselves is becoming increasingly sophisticated. As a result, many countries have become less inclined to turn a blind eye to violation of immigration laws.

Rather than relying on each individual country subsidiary to obtain the necessary visas and work permits, most major multinationals contract with a global immigration service provider or tax firm to manage the process. This step appears to be the best way of establishing a globally consistent and well-coordinated immigration process to support relocating assignees. HR managers need to be proactive, however, in briefing business managers and assignees on how long the process is likely to take and ensuring that they understand the potential consequences of violating immigration laws.

Cross-Cultural Training
During the last 20 years, there has been a rapidly increasing realization among multinationals of the importance of providing intercultural training to assignees, spouses/partners, and, often, their children prior to an international assignment. Typically, specialized service providers conduct this training, although a number of companies develop and administer their own programs internally.

The intent of such preparation is to introduce the assignee (and usually the spouse/partner) to the new host location. A significant number of companies also make the training available to qualified, accompanying dependent children.

The programs generally last two days and include information on living in the new host location, communicating across cultures, dealing with culture shock, adapting to the situation, and conducting busi-

Cross-Cultural Training

Who is eligible for cross-cultural training?

	% of companies
• Expatriate	68%
• Spouse	57%
• Family	38%

ORC 2008 Worldwide Policies and Practices Survey—930 participants
Copyright © 2008, ORC Worldwide

ness in the host country. The intercultural training usually occurs prior to their departure. In fact, a number of companies stipulate the session as a company requirement for accepting a global assignment.

Although expensive, cross-cultural training programs are invaluable in helping to minimize the risk of culture shock and demoralization when the assignee and family arrive at the host location. However (as discussed later in this book), it is equally important to provide well-organized orientation and settling-in support services on arrival at the host location. As one expatriate remarked: "It was very nice of the company to arrange a two-day session for our family on the history and customs of Switzerland before we moved to Zurich, but I wish someone had explained to us how to find the bank and post office and how to get a driver's license!"

Housing

One of the most emotional and challenging issues with any international assignment is the type of housing the assignee and family will receive in the host country and, if they are homeowners, what assistance to provide for their primary residence in the home country. Inadequate, inconsistent guidelines inevitably lead to bitter disputes and morale problems with assignees and families.

Virtually all multinationals assist assignees with the cost of housing at the host location. The most common approach followed by at least 60 percent of multinationals* is for the company to pay the assignee's actual foreign housing costs within approved cost guidelines. Some companies alternatively provide cash housing allowances, with other companies varying their practice by location. (* *ORC 2008 Worldwide Policies and Practices Survey.*)

To keep expenses under control, employers generally establish rental cost guidelines at the assignment location based on job level and family size. An example of this approach is shown below.

Once the expatriate finds suitable housing, a common approach is for the company to arrange the lease in the company's name and pay the rent directly. An advantage of this approach is that a number of countries (e.g., Singapore, Japan) provide favorable tax treatment when housing is provided as a benefit-in-kind.

Policies regarding the reimbursement of utilities (e.g., gas, electricity, water) at the assignment location vary considerably. About 90 percent of U.S. multinationals and over 50 percent of European multinationals reimburse utility costs, although most impose some cost limit. (*ORC 2008 Worldwide Policies and Practices Survey*). Establishing a cap is a

Sample Custom Housing Matrix - Geneva, Switzerland			
Annual Salary	Family Size 1	Family Size 2	Family Size 3+
Manager/ Professional	Housing Type: Apartment Bedrooms: 2	Housing Type: Apartment Bedrooms: 2 - 3	Housing Type: Apartment Bedrooms: 3 - 4
City/Area: Acacias Jonction Meyrin Plainpalais Servette	Average Rental Amount: CHF 2,200 - 3,200 Utilities: CHF 270	Average Rental Amount: CHF 3,000 - 4,200 Utilities: CHF 385	Average Rental Amount: CHF 4,400 - 6,000 Utilities: CHF 435
Director	Housing Type: Apartment Bedrooms: 2	Housing Type: Apartment Bedrooms: 2 - 3	Housing Type: Apartment Bedrooms: 3 - 4
City/Area: Carouge Chene-Bourg Eaux Vives Paquis Thonex	Average Rental Amount: CHF 3,200 - 4,800 Utilities: CHF 270	Average Rental Amount: CHF 4,400 - 6,200 Utilities: CHF 385	Average Rental Amount: CHF 6,000 - 7,500 Utilities: CHF 435
Executive	Housing Type: Apartment Bedrooms: 2	Housing Type: Apartment Bedrooms: 2 - 3	Housing Type: Apartment Bedrooms: 3 - 4
City/Area: Centre Champel Cologny Florissant Malagnou Vandoeuvres	Average Rental Amount: CHF 4,800 - 6,400 Utilities: CHF 270	Average Rental Amount: CHF 6,400 - 8,500 Utilities: CHF 385	Average Rental Amount: CHF 8,400 - 10,500 Utilities: CHF 435

wise move as stories abound of assignees running up outrageous bills, for example, by leaving swimming pools heated all winter!

Many companies expect assignees to contribute toward the cost of housing through deduction of an amount that is approximately equivalent to a typical housing expenditure in the home country (the home-housing norm). Deducted from the assignee's base salary during the assignment, the home-housing norm generally represents what a typical individual or family pays for housing and utilities in the home country. If based on national expenditure government survey data, the norm will vary by family size and income level. Some companies deduct a flat percentage of income, while others base the deduction on what the expatriate actually spent on housing in the home country. However, the latter approach can lead to a great deal of individual negotiation.

The deduction of a housing norm can create a number of problems. For example, if expatriates retain their home-country residence and cannot cover home ownership costs by renting out the property, inevitable pressure falls on the employer to waive or reduce the housing norm. As a result, according to ORC's 2008 *Worldwide Policies and Practices Survey*, 49 percent of European multinationals pay for host-country housing and do not deduct a housing norm. A growing number of U.S. multinationals (33 percent) follow the same practice.

Home-Sale Assistance

Does your company provide home-sale assistance to employees who chose to sell their homes?

	% of companies		
	Europe	Japan	U.S.
Yes	9%	6%	36%
Case by case	8%	5%	17%
No	83%	89%	47%

ORC 2008 Worldwide Policies and Practices Survey—930 participants
Copyright © 2008, ORC Worldwide

But helping expatriates sell their homes can also prove extremely expensive. The cost implications for companies in providing financial assistance to homeowners if they decide to sell their primary residence in the home country can be staggering, particularly with falling property values, whereby the company has to deal with potential losses on sale. U.S. multinationals have traditionally been more willing to provide home-sale assistance to assignees than European and Japanese multinationals, as can be seen from ORC survey data.

The cost of providing home-sale assistance is one of the reasons for the increasing trend among U.S. multinationals toward eliminating the housing-norm contribution. In return for providing "free housing" at the assignment location, those companies generally take a "hands-off" approach to the assignee's home-country housing obligations while on assignment and eliminate any provision for home-sale assistance.

For assignees who try to rent out their primary residence in the home country, companies that deduct a housing-norm contribution have to decide to what extent they are willing to assist assignees with issues such as property management fees, rental losses, and maintenance costs. As this administrative effort can often become costly and time-consuming

Home-Management Assistance

If you deduct a housing norm, how does your company assist employees who retain their homes while on assignment?

	% of companies
Pays property-management fees	51.6%
Pays some or all maintenance costs	15.4%
Manages rental of employee's home	11.2%
Pays rent if house becomes vacant	7.1%
Case by case assistance	14.7%
No assistance	25.3%

ORC 2008 Worldwide Policies and Practices Survey—312 respondents
Copyright © 2008, ORC Worldwide

for the company, many multinationals outsource property management services to third-party relocation firms. The level of support provided by multinationals varies considerably, as can be seen from the following data from ORC's 2008 *Worldwide Policies and Practices Survey* regarding the home-housing support policies of the 312 companies that do deduct a housing norm from their assignees.

Finally, what happens if assignees retain their primary residence while on assignment and are repatriated to a different location by the company? In those cases, companies typically provide home-sale assistance under their domestic relocation policies for their existing home and home-purchase assistance at the new location.

Autos

For many international moves, particularly between different continents, it can be very expensive and complex for assignees to take their personal cars. As a result, companies need to develop policies to deal with the disposal of personal cars in the home country and provide assistance with transportation needs in the country of assignment.

Sale of Personally Owned Autos. The majority of companies provide financial assistance with losses incurred by assignees that are forced to sell one (possibly two) personal cars in the home country when they relocate. If assignees eventually purchase one or more cars in the host country, the employer may also provide similar assistance if they have to sell those cars at the end of the assignment. It is also sensible to limit the loss on sale the company will reimburse; 20 percent of the retail price is a fairly common limit, as in the following example:

Auto Current Retail Value: $25,000
Actual Sale Price:. $18,000
Loss on Sale: $7,000
Limitation—20% of Retail Value: $5,000
Actual Reimbursement by Company $5,000

Alternatively, if the assignee leased the car, most companies provide assistance with cancellation fees, generally up to a predetermined limit.

Host-Country Transportation Assistance. The type of transportation assistance provided to assignees at different assignment locations can become a complex and sometimes emotional issue. Due to varying company cultures and differences in company car policies between countries, considerable variation exists in the level and type of transportation assistance in the host country. The first issue to be decided is whether or not to provide the assignee with a company car. As can be seen from the following survey data, practices vary widely.

If the assignee is a senior manager, there is a somewhat greater tendency to provide a company car. Certainly among U.S. multinationals, however, provision of company cars to assignees frequently meets with top management resistance as most companies do not provide company cars in the United States.

If the assignee does not receive a company car in the host country, there remains the issue as to what assistance, if any, to give the assignee toward the purchase or lease of a personal car. Typical policies include payment of car allowances, car leasing or rental assistance, and interest-free or low-interest loans. If the assignee's family is also at the assignment location, they generally need a second personal car. About 75 percent of employers do not provide any financial assistance

Company Cars & Car Allowances

Does your company provide a car or car allowance to expatriates at the assignment location?

	% of companies
• Yes, always	37%
• Yes, only if local practice for comparable positions	30%
• Yes, but only if job requires a car	13%
• Yes, if expatriate had a company car in home country	8%
• No	11%

ORC 2008 Worldwide Policies and Practices Survey—930 participants
Copyright © 2008, ORC Worldwide

for a second car, but 25 percent provide different types and levels of assistance.

Shipment and Storage of Household Goods
Companies normally engage the services of one or more relocation firms to ensure that the shipment of personal effects and household goods is managed in a consistent and cost-effective manner, rather than allow assignees to find their own vendors. So that the relocation process works effectively on a global basis, a number of critical actions are necessary:

1. Establish a formal policy outlining the amount of household goods the company is willing to have shipped to the assignment location. The basis for guidelines often involves shipping container size, for example:

   "The company will ship basic furniture needs based on the size of the rental property at the host location. The company will ship those items that will make the host location residence comfortable, provided such items fit into a standard 40-foot shipping container (12.2 m x 2.4 m x 2.6 m) for a family with children, and a standard 20-foot container (6.1 m x 2.4 m x 2.6 m) for a single assignee or couple."

2. Develop clear policy guidelines regarding the items for which the company will cover the shipping cost and those that are either not allowed or that can only be shipped at the assignee's personal expense. Typically, companies allow assignees to ship most household furniture, furnishings, and appliances that are part of a reasonable, normal household in the home country and that they will need on assignment. However, most employers typically prohibit items such as firearms and wine collections. Similarly, it is important to clarify the type of possessions for which the company will not pay shipping. It is not unheard of for companies to be confronted with requests to ship boats, trailers, hot tubs, motorcycles, and even horses! In these situations, it is important to have policy guidelines clearly stipulating that such major items will only be shipped if the assignee accepts responsibility for all shipping costs, insurance, and import duties.

3. Arrange for a survey by a moving company representative prior to the move to determine packing material and container requirements.

This step allows agreement on which items will be shipped to the host location, identification of articles that require special handling or packing, and items to be placed in storage for the duration of the assignment.

4. Allow assignees and their families to air ship limited personal effects they may need while waiting for the ocean shipment to arrive. A fairly typical policy would state: "You and your spouse are entitled to a maximum total air shipment of 300 pounds, plus 75 pounds for each qualified dependent who will be residing at the host location. This air shipment should be limited to clothing, special medical needs, baby needs, and toys for young children."

5. Decide on a clear policy regarding pets! As this issue can become very emotional, it is important to establish and communicate the assistance the company will provide for transporting and possibly quarantining pets, what type of pets, and how many.

6. Arrange for storage of household goods or personal effects that will not be shipped to the host location. However, it is advisable to limit the quantity of items, as storage of household goods can be very costly. Some companies provide incentives to dispose of items that will probably not be needed in the future or are just not worth storing.

7. Establish a limit on the amount of items the company will pay to ship back at the end of the assignment. For example, imposing a 10 percent limit on shipping the additional items purchased in the host location can avoid costly surprises when the assignee repatriates.

Relocation Allowance

One of the issues faced by companies during the international relocation process is how to deal with the myriad miscellaneous minor expenses incurred by expatriates and their families. Reimbursing the costs incurred for small appliances, driver's license fees, phone installation, and so on can become an administrative nightmare if these items have to be handled and approved separately. As a result, it is common practice to provide a lump-sum relocation allowance to cover most miscellaneous incidental expenses. Employers frequently base the allowance on a percentage of salary (e.g., one month's salary) or pay a flat amount.

While the intention is good, issues do arise because of the significant differences in the price of items between locations. For example, an allowance of $7,500 may be sufficient in the United States, but totally inadequate to purchase the same items in Tokyo. As a result, a number of companies have started to adjust the allowance level according to the relative costs of different assignment locations.

The following list represents typical items that are theoretically covered by a lump-sum relocation allowance:

- Passport fees and pictures.
- Traveler's check fees.
- Any special clothing needs, especially if there are major climate differences.
- Minor appliances and electronics.
- Window treatments, painting, decorating.
- International and host-country driver's licenses.
- Registration and license plate for one vehicle.
- Pet transport and immunization (all costs associated with relocating pets).
- Personal items (e.g., shaver, hair dryer).
- Telephone and cable television installation.
- Start-up grocery allowance.
- Preparation of will and power of attorney.

Temporary Living

Temporary living expenses for the assignee and family both in the home country prior to departure and in the host country while awaiting arrival of household goods can become very costly and need careful management. As it can often be logistically difficult for the assignee and family to be able to move directly from their residence in the home country to the assignment location, they may need to stay in a hotel or service apartment while making final arrangements for the move. Companies normally try to limit the period to no more than 15 or possibly 30 days, depending on the circumstances. A similar situation is likely to occur once the assignee and family arrive at the assignment location while waiting for the household goods shipment. To contain the costs, companies normally arrange for them to stay in a service apartment and reimburse the costs for a specified period, typically up to 30 days or possibly longer if there are delays with the shipment or in being able to move into longer-term rental housing.

While the majority of employers reimburse all temporary living expenses incurred by the assignee and family, some companies reimburse expenses only up to a specified limit, and others provide a flat per diem or cost-of-living allowance. The employer also reimburses car rental expenses if necessary during the period of temporary accommodations.

Destination Services

One of the most common complaints among assignees is lack of orientation and settling-in assistance when they arrive at the host location. Frequently, companies leave assignees on their own to handle matters such as finding information about banks, stores, doctors, mail, driver's licenses, and so on. Some companies may ask an employee to help the newly arrived family with their relocation on an ad hoc basis. Unfortunately, without experienced resources, assignees and their families can easily waste a great deal of time, make wrong decisions, and become very frustrated and disillusioned.

Increasingly, however, companies are using professional destination services firms to assist relocating assignees. These firms generally provide

Temporary Living

How are expenses handled for temporary living?

	% of companies	
	In home country	In host country
• All actual expenses reimbursed	40%	49%
• Reimbursed up to a set limit	25%	26%
• Covered in a per diem	8%	10%
• Cost-of-living allowance provided	1%	7%
• Expenses not covered	20%	2%

ORC 2008 Worldwide Policies and Practices Survey—930 participants
Copyright © 2008, ORC Worldwide

a comprehensive range of settling-in services—finding a home, negotiating a lease, arranging for utilities, helping to find local services (banks, doctors, autos, shops, appliances, expatriate clubs), scheduling school interviews, and providing help and advice on the myriad relocation issues encountered by assignees and their families. As many destination services providers are affiliated with worldwide relocation firms, multinationals can establish global contracts with relocation firms to provide a consistent range of services in most or all assignment locations. These services are usually not overly expensive, and the investment pays for itself by enabling assignees to be "up and running" in their new position as quickly as possible.

Family Support

Dual-Career Support

For potential assignees, the high incidence of dual-career situations creates major challenges for the employee, spouse/partner, and company. Because of the complexity of finding suitable employment in the host country, as well as trying to obtain a work visa, many employees turn down the chance of an international assignment or ask to go abroad on a single-status basis, with the spouse/partner and family remaining in the home country.

Very few companies are willing to provide financial compensation for the potential salary loss incurred by an accompanying spouse/part-

Dual Career/Spousal Assistance		
Does your company have a dual career/spousal assistance policy?		
	% of companies	
	North American	European
• Yes	43%	46%
• No, but intend to develop a policy	6%	9%
• No	51%	45%
ORC 2008 Worldwide Policies and Practices Survey—930 participants Copyright © 2008, ORC Worldwide		

ner. The cost of doing so could be very substantial, and the company might still be left with a professionally bored, demotivated spouse/partner at the assignment location. To find more appropriate solutions for dual-career problems, employers have taken a number of different approaches:

- Increasing the use of short-term, unaccompanied assignments of 3-12 months.
- Allowing employees to go on assignment as a "commuter," with the family remaining in the home country and trips home provided on a regular basis.
- Working with organizations such as the Permits Foundation, whose mission is to encourage governments to relax work permit regulations that currently make it difficult for spouses to work in many countries.
- Establishing policies that reimburse accompanying spouses unable to work in the assignment location for such costs as tuition, job placement, membership fees in professional organizations, seminars, and other career-related expenses. The objective is to enhance spouses' time in the host location by allowing them to maintain career interests. Most companies limit the amount they will reimburse, which can range from a flat amount of, say, $5,000 for the total assignment to as much as $5,000 per year. Although these policies in no way replace the loss of earnings, assignees and spouses/partners generally regard them in a positive light, with the company perceived as at least recognizing the problem and offering some level of assistance.

Education

Although international assignment policies can vary significantly with regard to compensation and allowances, one policy area with remarkable consistency among multinationals is that of children's education. Virtually all multinationals contribute to the cost of international or private school for assignee children from kindergarten through high school.

Typically, companies reimburse tuition, textbooks, and transportation for children to attend an international or private school at the host location, with the family expected to cover expenses related to optional activities and school outings. The cost of subsidizing education can be staggeringly high for the company, ranging from $15,000 to $25,000 annually, depending on the location. Nevertheless, companies have learned that employees with school-age children will rarely accept an assignment if they are concerned that their children's education will be disrupted, so educational expenses have become an accepted part of the assignment process. The only major exception involves assignments to the United States, where there is generally company pressure to have the children attend public schools.

In certain cases, the host-country school may advise the need for special or additional tutoring to bridge any shortfalls between the home-country curriculum and the new host-country school requirements to allow children to integrate more easily into the new assignment country's educational system. For example, special training might include additional language lessons if most classes are not in the child's native tongue. Companies invariably cover these types of costs.

In host locations where the company considers both public and private schools inadequate, the employer normally provides an allowance to assist with expenses incurred when the student remains in the family's home country for grammar school or high school studies, or attends school in a location other than the host or home country. In these situations, companies establish a maximum subsidy to help cover tuition, room, board, and certain required expenses.

In addition to an education allowance, students that attend schools outside the host country can generally take two round trips per year to visit their family. Companies rarely provide an allowance to assist assignees with the expense of educating a student

Children's Education	
For what levels of formalized education will your company contribute to educational expenses?	
	% of companies
• Preschool	45%
• Kindergarten	91%
• Primary school	97%
• Secondary school	98%

ORC 2008 Worldwide Policies and Practices Survey—930 participants
Copyright © 2008, ORC Worldwide

at the college or university level, but they typically reimburse either one or two economy roundtrip airfares per school year from school to the host location.

Language Training

Having the ability to converse in the host-country language is one of the key factors in enabling the assignee and family to adapt successfully to the assignment location. Most multinationals arrange for and pay reasonable costs for the assignee and spouse/partner to take intensive language lessons when transferring to a country where their native language is not spoken. If possible, the classes should begin in the home country to allow them to at least manage a few words and phrases in the local language on arrival. Although companies generally establish an initial limit on the number of lesson hours (e.g., 100 hours), they frequently extend this period if the assignee and spouse/partner make good progress and are motivated to continue studying.

Dealt with separately, most children receive language training as part of the school curriculum at the host location. However, if additional tutoring is necessary, employers handle it on a case-by-case basis.

Home Leave

For assignees whose families accompany them, over 80 percent of companies provide at least one home leave annually for the whole family. The official intent of an annual home leave trip is to enable the assignee and family to maintain personal and professional ties to their home location. However, companies frequently find themselves under pressure from assignees to permit them to spend their "home leave" in a location other than their home country. The majority of companies allow this option, even though subsidizing

Home Leave

Does your company require that expatriates spend their home leave in their home country?

	% of companies
Yes	58%
No	42%

ORC 2008 Worldwide Policies and Practices Survey—930 participants
Copyright © 2008, ORC Worldwide

a vacation (say, in Fiji) is hardly likely to help maintain professional contacts in the home country that may prove critical when trying to find a suitable position upon repatriation.

Another approach taken by about 16-18 percent of North American and European companies to simplify administration and avoid arguments as to whether a vacation in Fiji constitutes home leave is to provide a lump-sum payment in lieu of home-leave travel for assignees to use as they wish.

Class of travel is another critical and costly issue regarding home leave. At least 75 percent of companies reimburse economy air fares only for home-leave trips, although about a third reimburse business class airfares for particularly long flights (e.g., at least eight or nine hours). An example of a "typical" home-leave policy is shown below:

Home Leave For...	Provisions
Single and accompanied assignees.	The company will reimburse actual nonrefundable airfare tickets for one home-leave trip per year for you and your accompanying family members, using a direct return trip from the assignment location to the home location. You may use this trip only for travel between the assignment and home locations. For trips with a total actual flying time exceeding 10 hours, you may elect to fly business class. For trips with a total actual flying time of less than 10 hours, the company will reimburse coach class only.
Unaccompanied assignees.	If you go on assignment while your family remains in the home location, the company will reimburse actual ticket costs for four trips per year, using a direct return trip from the assignment location to the home location at the most cost-effective nonrefundable coach class fare. Alternatively, your spouse may use the home leave benefit to travel to the assignment location. Trips can be exchanged on a one-to-one basis.

Rest and Recreation Leave
In addition to annual home leave, a number of companies provide additional leave for the assignee and family when they are based in particularly difficult assignment locations. This leave typically takes the form of a five-to-seven-day expenses-paid trip for the assignee and family to a "non-hardship" location in the same region. For example, the company might provide an annual rest and recreation (R&R) trip to a western European capital for those assigned to a remote location in Russia, or a trip to Hong Kong or Singapore for assignees in a remote Chinese location. U.S. multinationals are usually more likely to provide this benefit than European or Asian multinationals.

How do employers determine which hardship locations qualify for R&R trips? Depending on the methodology used, hardship ratings typically vary from 5 to 40 percent, depending on the severity of local conditions. Companies that provide R&R trips for selected locations might, for example, do so only for those with at least a 20 percent hardship rating (e.g., Tripoli, Libya or La Paz, Bolivia). In extreme cases (e.g., Angola, Zimbabwe) that carry hardship ratings of at least 30 percent, some companies may provide two annual R&R leaves.

Vacation and Holidays
Home-country vacation policies vary widely, from two weeks' entitlement for some U.S. employees to six weeks for many German employees. This variance creates a dilemma when companies send employees of different nationalities on assignment, especially those sent to countries whose employees have much higher vacation entitlements than in their home country.

Company policies also vary considerably, with about half keeping assignees on their home-country vacation policies. Others try to bridge the policy differences in various ways, for example, by basing entitlements on home-country policies, but guaranteeing a minimum of 20 days' vacation on assignment.

The normal practice for public holidays is for assignees to observe the same holidays as do local employees in the host location. If assignees also

Vacation Policies	
Which of the following best describes your company's vacation policy for expatriates?	
	% companies
• Vacation according to home-country policy	51%
• Vacation according to host-country policy	27%
• Higher of home- or host-country entitlement	12%
• Home-country policy plus additional time	10%
ORC 2008 Worldwide Policies and Practices Survey—930 participants	
Copyright © 2008, ORC Worldwide	

wish to observe certain home-country holidays, employers usually expect them to use part of their vacation entitlement to do so.

Health Care

There are two critical priorities with regard to health care for assignees and their families—ensuring that health issues are identified and properly addressed prior to the relocation and providing comprehensive coverage during the assignment.

Medical Examinations. Many companies make the assignment offer contingent upon the potential assignee and spouse/partner passing a medical examination prior to departure. The purpose of the examination and associated medical tests is to identify any health risks and treatment needed before taking up residence in the host country. If the assignee has dependent children who will reside at the host location, the company generally encourages them to also undergo a medical examination prior to the move and bears the cost of examinations and required immunizations. During the assignment, most companies encourage and reimburse the costs of yearly medical examinations for the assignee and family members residing at the host location.

Providing Comprehensive Health Care on Assignment. With the rapidly increasing numbers of different assignee nationalities and locations, providing consistent health care is a significant challenge. While retaining assignees in their home-country medical insurance plans is certainly one

Health Care	
What health care coverage does your company provide to expatriates and their families?	
	% companies
• Home-country plan	19%
• Home-country plan with extra coverage added	20%
• Assignment-location plan	9%
• International health care plan	52%
ORC 2008 Worldwide Policies and Practices Survey—930 participants Copyright © 2008, ORC Worldwide	

option, not all plans provide comprehensive worldwide coverage, which can force companies to find ad hoc solutions when problems arise. Even if the home-country plan provides full coverage, the insurance provider may not have the expertise and administrative systems to deal with complicated claims submitted by assignees in different languages and terminology.

As a result, a significant number of multinationals enroll assignees in global health care plans provided by organizations such as Cigna International, Aetna, and Bupa International. These organizations provide comprehensive global health insurance programs that can be customized to client needs, along with dedicated, multilingual staff available 24/7 to assist with benefit verification, payment guarantees, and physician and hospital referrals. Such plans are not inexpensive, but do ensure peace of mind to assignees, their families, and the HR managers responsible for them.

Career Planning—During Assignment

Whenever assignee satisfaction surveys are conducted, the most common complaint involves lack of communication and repatriation planning. To quote one assignee: "I spent the first year of my assignment trying to settle into the new location. It was only during the second year that I was really able to be productive, and my third and last year was spent trying to find a suitable job once I repatriated." Despite their massive financial investment in assignees, companies face challenges in avoiding the assignee perception that they are "out of sight, out of mind." Consequently, employers implement different solutions to counter this phenomenon, such as:

- Appointing a career mentor who will keep in touch with the expatriate throughout the assignment, from pre-departure to post-return. Ideally, this individual should be a senior executive in the same business or functional area as the assignee, and, if possible, have had international assignment experience. The challenge for the company is to find someone able to commit to mentoring for the length of the assignment.

- Ensuring that assignees receive annual performance appraisals, which are typically conducted by the host-country manager. However, if the assignee has a "dotted-line" relationship to a manager in the home country, too, that individual should also provide input.

- Incorporating assignees into corporate succession planning programs. All too often, assignees find themselves "forgotten" and not included in these types of reviews.

- Organizing a top management review board that meets, for example, every six months and reviews reports on assignee performance and plans for repatriation or next assignment. Companies that have been able to institutionalize such top management involvement in the career planning process for assignees have achieved a much higher degree of management and organizational accountability for the long-term success of their assignment programs.

Other approaches to help assignees stay in touch with their home-country business organization include:

- Ensuring that assignees remain on the distribution lists for company publications that may normally have more of a domestic, home-country circulation.

- Recommending that assignees visit their home-country headquarters while on home leave.

- Encouraging senior business leaders to meet with assignees whenever they visit international locations.

- Establishing internal job posting systems that can be accessed globally to enable assignees to look for opportunities upon repatriation.

Emergencies

Security Precautions
Since September 11, 2001, the need for companies to implement
security precautions and potential evacuation procedures for assignees,
their families, and international business travelers has become crucial.
One of the most essential precautions is to insist that assignees and
business travelers provide contact information at all times in case of
emergency. Likewise, many companies have established security monitoring services that assignees and business travelers can contact 24/7
globally in case of emergencies (e.g., serious car accidents, injury or
illness requiring hospitalization, violent crime, or terrorist attack).

Prior to both short- and long-term international assignments, it is
essential to provide security briefings to assignees and their families.
Unfortunately, briefings do not always occur, which can clearly result
in assignees and their families inadvertently stumbling into hazardous
situations.

Most companies have introduced (or are in the process of introducing)
a range of new security measures according to ORC's surveys.

According to Control Risks Group, one of the leading global consulting firms in the field of risk consulting, best practice in travel and
expatriate risk management means:

Security	
What new security measures has your company introduced?	
	% companies
• Introduced or improved evacuation procedures	66%
• Introduced or improved security briefings	63%
• Improved security in all locations	49%
• Introduced assignment tracking systems	26%
ORC 2008 Worldwide Policies and Practices Survey—930 participants Copyright © 2008, ORC Worldwide	

- Preparing your people for travel and preparing your organization to support them.
- Tracking personnel and maintaining the capability to identify where they are at any point.
- Monitoring risk levels and informing staff and managers in a timely fashion of developing threats.
- Providing advice and local support when necessary.
- Being prepared to respond quickly should you need to get them out of danger.

Medical Emergencies
When multinationals establish facilities in remote areas where medical care may be lacking, the need for assignees and business travelers to have access to emergency medical support in the event of serious illness or accident becomes essential. As a result, companies frequently contract with global health care and assistance companies (e.g., International SOS, MEDEX) to provide emergency medical support services for their employees worldwide. For example, International SOS has a network of more than 2,000 professionals in alarm centers, available 24/7. This service includes access to international clinics and remote-site medical facilities across five continents, with medical and technical support services available in more than 30 languages.

Multinationals generally contract with international emergency medical services organizations primarily to address the following services for international business travelers and global assignees:
- Referrals to primary care physicians, physician specialists, hospitals, and dentists.
- Emergency and routine medical advice by a physician.
- Travel-related information, including immunization recommendations, U.S. State Department travel advisories, and locations of embassies, consulates, and so on.
- Advice regarding whether specific prescription medication is available locally.
- Arrangement of medical evacuation and guarantee of payment to providers.

Serious Illness or Death in Family

One of the unfortunate contingencies for which companies have to develop policies is the possibility of death or serious illness of a family member while on assignment. To avoid having to deal with what can be highly emotional situations on an ad hoc basis, it is important to establish policy guidelines as to which family members will be covered, how much leave time will be granted, and what transportation assistance will be provided. The following is an example of a typical policy covering death or illness of a family member:

Death or Illness of Family Member.

Limited paid time off is permitted for the serious illness or death of your spouse, child, parent, sister, or brother. In the event of a death, normal time off is up to 15 days, plus travel time; for serious illness, up to seven days plus travel time. Additional days are charged against accrued vacation. Transportation (round trip airfare) is only reimbursable from the host location to your home-country location. All other expenses are your personal financial responsibility.

At the discretion of the host-location manager, round trip transportation may be allowed for both you and your spouse in the event of a death in either of your immediate families.

Transportation For...	In the Event of...
Assignee	Death or serious illness of spouse, mother, father, brother, or sister.
Spouse	Death or serious illness of mother, father, brother, or sister.
Assignee or Spouse	Serious illness of a child not residing at the host location.
Assignee, Spouse, and Children	Death of a child not residing at the host location.

Employee Assistance Programs

Family problems, especially the inability of family members to adapt successfully, represent the most common causes of international assignment failure. Cross-cultural training and well-organized orientation and settling-in services can help families deal with the stresses of a new and generally very strange environment. However, companies are increasingly recognizing the need to provide ongoing third-party employee assistance programs (EAPs) during the entire assignment. Companies can contract with specialist global service providers such as SAIC and ComPsych to assign counselors who have experience in adapting to other cultures, understand a global assignee's issues, and have training in global assignee assistance needs. These individuals normally provide:

- Counseling for the assignee or family members at the host location in areas such as health and safety, aging parents, work-related issues, substance abuse, stress, adjustment, adolescent/child problems, marital problems, and so on.
- Response to crises at home and in the workplace.
- Availability to talk with the assignee and family at any time to discuss issues as they arise.

Discussions with the counselor are in strictest confidence, and each family member can contact his or her individual counselor at any time. Although these programs are voluntary, employers encourage all global assignees and their families to participate.

Repatriation

Finding the Right Position
Despite the best intentions, very few companies are able to guarantee assignees a suitable position—or even a position at all—upon repatriation.

The responsibility for helping assignees find a job within the company upon repatriation is very often unclear. Assignee surveys typically illustrate this confusion, with responses as to who is responsible for helping them to find their next position ranging from their home-country manager, home-country HR manager, and assignees themselves. Very few companies have a centralized, well-coordinated process for providing career management and repatriation placement

Repatriation	
Does your company guarantee a job on repatriation?	
	% companies
• Yes, employment at the same level	18%
• Yes, but depends on what jobs are available	35%
• No, company does not guarantee a job	46%

ORC 2008 Worldwide Policies and Practices Survey—930 participants
Copyright © 2008, ORC Worldwide

assistance. All too often, assignees end up in temporary holding positions when they return home or terminated because the company has nothing suitable to offer them.

Nevertheless, many companies actively try to implement programs to ensure that assignees find appropriate jobs upon repatriation to avoid losing valuable talent and the company's major investment in an international assignment. However, the employer needs to establish effective programs—career mentors, annual performance appraisals, inclusion of assignees in corporatewide succession planning, top management global assignment review boards—as key elements within the global mobility process in order to be successful.

The positive news is that a growing number of companies are merging their international assignment administration groups into global talent management functions to make sure that assignees do not "fall between the cracks." The greatest guarantee of success for any global mobility program is when the company moves repatriated employees into highly visible positions. This action demonstrates the value that the company places on experience gained through international assignments and encourages other high potential individuals to make sure their names are considered for possible assignments.

Settling-in Support
"Returning expatriates and their families often come home with an unrealistic set of expectations that lead to confusion and disappointment

on re-entry," says Rita Bennett in her chapter on International Assignment Issues in *The International Human Resources Guide,* published by Thomson West. "On a personal level, most assignees and their accompanying family members report that they have experienced a tremendous amount of personal growth while living internationally. It is often frustrating and disillusioning for repatriates to discover that it is difficult to integrate their new attitudes, skills, and knowledge into their home environment and that their family, friends, and colleagues are not always interested in their international experiences."

In many cases, assignees and their families are staggered to find that adapting back to their home-country culture and relationships can be just as challenging as the cultural adaptation challenges they experienced when first moving to the host country. While on assignment, expatriates tend to remember the positive aspects of their previous home-country life and forget the negatives they are now forced to deal with again. As a result, a growing number of companies have instituted programs to help assignees and families with the adjustment process after they repatriate, such as:

- Offering repatriation counseling and workshops so participants can identify changes that have taken place in themselves and in their home country while on assignment, as well as openly discuss the re-entry problems they are experiencing and develop plans to adapt back into their home-country culture.
- Implementing career assistance programs to the spouse/partner, similar to those offered at the start of an international assignment (e.g., career counseling, job search assistance, resume writing, other types of job placement support).
- Providing opportunities for returning assignees to use their newly acquired international skills, such as sharing their international experience within the organization through internal briefing sessions on lessons learned, counseling potential new assignees, and participating in international task forces or project teams.

Evaluating Assignment Results
Despite the high cost of global assignments, very few companies use any type of performance metric to assess the impact international assign-

ments are having on assignees' careers. In a survey on *Global Mobility Program Management*, conducted in 2007 by ORC Worldwide and Deloitte among 377 North American and European multinationals, more than 80 percent of the participants do not or cannot track what happens to assignees upon repatriation and over the years after their assignment. How many of these employees are promoted and how many leave the company, are questions to which many companies are unable to provide clear answers.

Only a small percentage of companies appear to have systems in place to track these statistics accurately. This fact is surprising in light of the fact that global mobility programs can represent very significant investments, financially and in terms of critical resources.

Companies frequently face challenges in trying to establish and track assignment program metrics. For example, once assignees repatriate, the international assignment administration group typically no longer has any responsibility for them, and assignees may transfer to a different payroll. Another contributory factor is that many companies have downsized or outsourced their international assignment administration, leaving very little time for remaining staff to assume this additional level of responsibility.

Ultimately, one of the most important means of evaluating the success or failure of any international assignment program is to ask the managers who employ the assignees whether they feel that their investment has been worthwhile. Assuming managers are willing to be candid and

---

Program Metrics

- 86 percent of companies are not tracking any form of program metrics.
- Of those companies that do track metrics, the most common statistics tracked include:
  » % of employees voluntarily leaving company while on assignment.
  » % of employees repatriating or taking new assignment at same job level.
  » % of failed assignments (assignee repatriation prior to assignment completion).
  » % of employees promoted during or at end of assignment.
  » % of employees voluntarily leaving company within three years of repatriation.

ORC & Deloitte 2007 Global Mobility Program Management Survey of 377 multinationals
Copyright © 2008, ORC Worldwide

respond honestly, this question is an obvious, fundamental one to ask. After all, these are the clients who bear the cost of the international program. Companies that do systematically seek feedback from their management clients consistently confirm that the feedback they receive is a crucial metric in evaluating the effectiveness of their assignment management process.

Conclusion

Being able to develop and manage global mobility programs that allow multinationals to source and deploy their best talent to support the organization's strategic business goals can give companies the key competitive edge they need. In a time of global economic turmoil and uncertainty, the strategic need for companies to be able to provide skilled resources wherever needed globally in the most cost-effective manner possible has become paramount. The intent of this booklet has been not only to describe many of the complex challenges involved in managing these programs but also to provide a blueprint of a range of practices that leading multinationals have found to be the most effective. We conclude with another very relevant quote from Jack Welch:

> *"Globalization has changed us into a company that searches the world, not just to sell or to source, but to find intellectual capital— the world's best talents and greatest ideas."*

Get recognized around the world.
Achieve the GPHR designation.

Achieving and maintaining the HR Certification Institute's Global Professional in Human Resources (GPHR®) credentials proves that you have mastered and can apply forward-thinking international HR practices, policies

and procedures that HR professionals are expected to know in order to perform their jobs effectively.

Choosing to obtain your GPHR credentials is a career-long commitment that demonstrates that you are driven to be successful in international HR management.

Earning your GPHR credentials can:
* Increase your professional confidence because you have validated that you know and can apply the core global HR practices.
* Set you apart from your peers when applying for new professional opportunities.
* Result in greater respect from the organization in which you work.

The GPHR certification is valued throughout the HR industry in the United States and abroad because the exams test knowledge gained from experience working in the global HR field. In addition, it provides a common HR language that is understood across the world.

Start your career-long commitment to setting a higher standard for yourself and achieve the GPHR credentials from the HR Certification Institute. Go to www.hrci.org to learn more.

Recommended SHRM Books

The Employer's Immigration Compliance Desk Reference
By Gregory Siskind

The EQ Interview: Finding Employees with High Emotional Intelligence
By Adele B. Lynn

HR Competencies: Mastery at the Intersection of People and Business
By Dave Ulrich, Wayne Brockbank, Dani Johnson, Kurt Sandholtz, and Jon Younger

Human Resource Transformation: Demonstrating Strategic Leadership in the Face of Future Trends
By William J. Rothwell, Robert K. Prescott, and Maria W. Taylor

Investing in People: Financial Impact of Human Resource Initiatives
By Wayne Cascio and John Boudreau

The Manager's Guide to HR: Hiring, Firing, Performance Evaluations, Documentation, Benefits, and Everything Else You Need to Know
By Max Muller

Outsourcing Human Resources Functions: How, Why, When, and When Not to Contract for HR Services, 2nd edition
By Mary F. Cook and Scott B. Gildner

Performance Appraisal Source Book: A Collection of Practical Samples
By Mike Deblieux

Solving the Compensation Puzzle: Putting Together a Complete Pay and Performance System
By Sharon K. Koss

Smart Policies for Workplace Technologies: Email, Blogs, Cell Phones & More
By Lisa Guerin

Strategic Staffing: A Comprehensive System for Effective Workforce Planning, 2nd edition
By Thomas P. Bechet

Weathering Storms: Human Resources in Difficult Times
By Society for Human Resource Management